The Oxford and Cambridge

may anthologies 2000

POETRY

Varsity/Cherwell

Varsity Publications Limited, 11-12 Trumpington Street, Cambridge CB2 1QA

Published by Varsity Publications Limited 2000

ISBN 0 902240 28 5

A CIP catalogue record for this book is available from the British Library

Typeset by Rachel Flowerday
Printed and bound in Great Britain by Origen Production Limited

Original concept: Peter Davies, Adrian Woolfson, Ron Dimant

Further copies of this book and others in the series can be obtained through all good bookshops or direct from Varsity Publications Limited, 11-12 Trumpington Street, Cambridge CB2 1QA.
Telephone: (44) 01223 353422
Fax: (44) 01223 352913
Email address: business@varsity.cam.ac.uk

Website: www.varsity.cam.ac.uk/Anthologies

may anthologies 2000

Editors: Sophie Levy (Cambridge)
Tom Rob Smith (Cambridge)
Catherine Shoard (Oxford)
Peter Robins (Oxford)

Executive Editor: Paul Muldoon

Publisher: Rachel Flowerday

Cover Design: Shehani Fernando, Rachel Flowerday

Cover Photos: Shehani Fernando

Editorial Committees

Prose: Matt Applewhite
Jo Goulbourne
Trisha Gupta
Maartje Scheltens
Debs Stansfield
Zoë Svendsen

Poetry: Sarah Cain
Ruth Fowler
Wendy Lee
Douglas McCabe
Betty Messazos

Selection co-ordinator: Ajesh Patalay

Launched 5th May 2000 at Waterstone's, Cambridge

Thanks

College sponsors

Cambridge:

Churchill, Clare, Darwin, Emmanuel, Fitzwilliam, Gonville & Caius, King's, Lucy Cavendish, Jesus, Newnham, Pembroke, Queens', Robinson, St. Catharine's, St. John's, Selwyn, Sidney Sussex, Trinity

Oxford:

Christ Church's Christopher Tower Fund, Hertford, Jesus, Linacre, Magdalen, Oriel, St. Peter's, The Queen's College

Thanks also to Carole Blake, Dr Michael Franklin, Lawrence Norfolk, Sophie Craig, Ben Yeoh, Jon Travers, Jill Hocking, Isobel Dixon, Phillip Wells, Adam and Liz at Waterstone's, Melony at Corpus Christi, Diana Tapp, Joti and Debbie, Graduate Advisers at Natwest, Ken Barnett & Origen Production Ltd and Suzanne Arnold for their assistance, and everyone who submitted work

contents

Contents

Introduction

It's been my great pleasure to take up the invitation to make this selection of poems written by students at the Universities of Cambridge and Oxford, though it was a somewhat perplexing business to reduce the longer short-list offered to me to a mere twenty poems.

As I read through that long short-list, I was reminded yet again of the extraordinary variety of ways in which poetry finds its way into the world. I was reminded even more forcibly, however, of one unvarying fact — that the much vaunted regard for the well-observed, concrete image, the arresting simile or metaphor, is much vaunted because these continue to be at the heart of almost all effective poems. I think of the details of the "black mould/ Hidden by fresh wet laundry" in **5 Haiku**, or the "I lap out like a wolfcub at the memory of you by my side" in **'A lupine sky.'**

Another constant here is a regard for the inconstancy of language, the delight in the slipping and sliding as words rearrange themselves into new orders. I think here of the description of **Lowenzahn (Dandelion)** "spoken yellow so taut/ and told in debris", of the student "thick as pigshit, mouthy with it" in **Subtraction**, of "the bacon frazzlies/ the lemon dazzlies" in **Mr Bancini opens his quaint little shop of bottles**.

I very much hope you'll have as much fun as I have reading the twenty "dazzlies," lemon or otherwise, collected here.

Paul Muldoon
(Professor of Poetry, University of Oxford)

Missa Brevis

Today, we can all be gondoliers
pushing down the shallow river in our straw hats.
There is only so much danger we can get ourselves
into, averting the banks and the low bridge
with our little paddles and ancient punting poles.
The geese, even the ones from Canada, are used to this;
with a squawk, they are gone before our boats
can touch them. The grass is much drier here in late
                                                    April
than we thought it could be, nearly dry enough to sit on
without checking our pants when we get up. The mallards
are making their way to the shore to mooch baguettes.
The last tulips are opening their red arms wider than
                                                    intended,
until they fall to the grass, but how can it be helped
in this warm weather? Lilacs, and hyacinths and the other
Greek flowers are reconsidering spring in their new
                                                    forms,
fearless and sweeter-smelling than beyond even their own
old wildest dreams. You can tell the Americans mostly
by the way they push off, like they're batting alligators,
though a few, like the French, are recumbent on the
                                                    boat-bottoms,
curled like petals, already dreaming of a river more
                                                    peaceful.

Michael Snediker

Opheliae

1

Saint Ophelia, virgin mother of those
   Ladies who love, sing, and drown,
Rests her mad head in a muddy repose,
    Smooths out her skirts and sinks down.
        Sing willow, willow, willow.

And this country maiden knows nothing of courts
  Yet here she is, bursting for breath.
What unknown, unheard, and unpitying thoughts
  Fill her as she sinks down to death?
        Sing willow, willow, willow.

Let Hamlet rave on, neither care for him now;
  And none of his boastings can wake her.
Over the Avon the willowtrees bow
  He prov'd mad, and did forsake her.

        The wild willows weep, the wan waters drench;
        It was always the way for the jilted wench.

II

Raining into the history books,
water soaks into her skirts;
euphemistic mud
slimes round her ankles.
She is walking.

When the damp
has reached the skin beneath this dress
and her limbs are waterlogged;
when wet as rivers could make her,
stone-heavy, stone-cold,
well then she'll haul
the dead weight of her body
over that railing
and fall.

Meanwhile there's something soothing
in this slow tread that travels nowhere;
the pace of an animal measuring its cage.
She counts her steps like sheep
before sleeping. A steady pavement
and, swirling below,
the rush of the turbulent Thames.

The boatmen set forth;
not knowing that tonight
they shall net strange fish.

Carolyn Smith

Miss Bankhead's Invitation to Dinner

I had seduced everyone from here to Times Square
and further. Well, everyone except for her.

So I prepared dinner for two, raw fish and candlelight.
I told her directions, I told her Tuesday night.

If Oppenheim was the Garbo of Montparnasse, then
                                        what was she?
Late. I expected her for two hours, gave up at three.

Then after ten, a chinese girl's shown in. Red lips, black
                                                    wig.
I look at her out of the corner of my eye. Like this.

Miss Garbo could no come but send me, Miss.
So we sit down. I watch her silver fingers mince the fish.

Then she bends over the oysters towards me.
The seams of my stockings. The edge of my seat.

And when it's over it's her own voice that says
(like butter) *Pleased to have met you Miss.*

Emily Haworth-Booth

Lowenzahn (Dandelion)

Fired up for all aspects
and shards found fully

spoken yellow so taut
and told in debris

the slip stream of let
it be and before and

reasoned fully distinct
if orange at struck disc

out by hubcap bird
caught as sign or distinguished

visitor as the legend doubtless
revives the juli konig

to remain indistinct
or angled or grand uprooted.

Leo Mellor

Mrs Mellors' Lost Lover

Love in a hut, with water and a crust
having to do for her ladyship's breakfast,
and afterwards walking her under the stars
as far as the gate, and watching her fade;
then the darkness's yawn, the breeze in the beeches,
and sleepless with feeling back at the cottage,
her belly's soft skin under his fingers,
the light of a hurricane-lamp in her hair.

And at dawn the leaves are blood-bronze, the air
pricks his lungs, he comes to the hut with a trap
and a clutch of primroses for the hearth;
in his nostrils the skeins of her scent tremble
like candleflames, while his fingertips seek out
her warmth in the rucks of the blanket,
the ghosts of her limbs in the space where she lay;
but at dusk she still hasn't come.

Three days and he knows that she won't;
still, when a twig snaps the saw bites his thumb;
for a second she kneels at the chopping-log,
he watches birds feed from the trough of her palm;
but she's gone, and he's tipping arsenic
in the corn-bin, scattering fistfuls of grain
in an arc round the hut; pheasants and hens
are pecking it out of the dust.

Sick of onions and beer, he upsets
the table and chair, and the wickered walls shake,
the lamp bursts on the floor, paraffin streaks
and catches, he turns his axe on the hen-coops,
his gun on the dog; a crescent moon leaks
into the furrows of the sky; in smirr
he sprints as far as the knoll, filling
with the lunacy of engine-noise, electric light.

Sam Gilbert

Mr Bancini opens his quaint little shop of bottles

with brilliantine brilloed hair
       and 1920's Green-grocer get-up

            he has the hour of his life...

...Ssspit the bacon-frazzlies

      the lemon dazzlies

the lemon-grasses

      chinese-style morning

         (with)

the streaky greens

         (of)

Spring

      Onion

a packet of Fuck-Bangs

         in My Hand

(bottles of hair gel)

a barber's pole

Lee Kern

Irredente

In my poem about Italy,
there is a piazza
with the sun striking the cobbles;
there is a fountain
(for water is a good thing to have in a poem)
and there is also, possibly, a sky.

My mother, nineteen, is in the second stanza;
sixties-skinny in a crochet bikini,
passing up Venice for a day on the beach.
Her friend hitchhikes home across Europe
because it is the summer of love, and she can.
My mother catches the appointed plane
and scarcely speaks to her again.

There is a hotel room,
cool and gloomy with old dark wood.
There are some Italian words
to add local colour.
I learn some for the melody,
the type of words you'd put in a poem:
sole, luna, stella, fiore,
notte, cielo, cuore…

You are not in it yet,
but I am hoping this will change.

This is my poem about Italy
which is waiting for me to go there
so it can be written.

Carolyn Smith

Love Song to a Photographer

Colour, water, wind, the air. These are
The lenses of your photographs and I
Have never modelled for you once. We stare
At them together in your darkest eye
Where I must clutch and search in water for
Impressions. You love edges and the sea
And, more than me, not knowing ever where
You are. The images fall flat and free
And light escapes from your bare hand, the shudder
Of the camera, spasm in your wrist,
In us. How you control what moves and if
It lives, and for how long! These days I wonder
When we'll lean against each other, kiss
By accident, to seek some proof of love.

Heather Clark

Ways to Tell if the Couple is Still Together

Or if, when the man leaves,
it is over. The woman
pulls her very white blond hair
into a new pony-tail. She orders
another Bacardi and Coke
when the waitress comes to take
their plates. And then, deciding moment,
when the dove is in sight, when the wind,
just a little, picks up in the sail, she moves
her hand to his plate, what has been left
of an airport restaurant salad, picks up,
between two fingers, an oily crouton.
They are professional ballroom dancers;
they're going to win the cha-cha.

Michael Snediker

At the Tate Gallery

The Yves Klein monochrome at the Tate is kept in a glass case, rendering it
impossible to focus upon due to reflections in the glass (the most prominent
of which was, when I saw it, Matisse's *Snail*).

7) Whereof one cannot speak, thereof one must be silent. — Ludwig Wittgenstein

Thereof daub in blue (IK)
and hang as baubles round.

Ludwig you were
vibrant enough of
hue to apprehend
the more there is
                 within
eyeshadow and skin
that must needs not be silent,
that will licentious sit
(or should that be 'will hang'?)
like blue pigment in resin.

Bluefaced waxgirl you
your glass case clasp
around and light refract.
I copy: look inward back
at hands, eyes (blue (IK)) —
[I K; I nearly care]
the phrase truncated, and
shouldn't there be
an 'about you'
somewhere about me?

listen me to
my borrowed blood,
tallow candle my
mothlight.
laugh me to
my borrowed aspect,
shadow,
        my shadow.

But you behave
as real objects ought
and reflect
        that cut-out snail
which reminds me of the glass
and the lines that crop
up.

Tom Perrin

Unos tiempos

Una esquiva esencia —
alquimistas tempranas trataron de destilarlo

con alambiques pero resbaló entre
sus manos como el pez mas pequeñito

a través de las redes — sin embargo cuando cogido
tiene el sentimiento contento de la arena debajo del pie.

Some Time

An elusive substance —
early alchemists tried to distil it

with alembics but it slipped through
their hands like the tiniest of fish

through nets — however when caught
has the satisfying feeling of sand under feet.

Ben Yeoh

5 Haiku

Kissing my new boyfriend

Skin flakes off my nose
His short beard is hard and coarse
Sore lips crave for more

Soaking in my bath

Ceiling with black mould
Hidden by fresh wet laundry
Dripping on my face

Running

Beautiful muscles
Gasp for air in agony
The smell of sweat

Melting Butter

Quick, lick grease off finger
Wipe in tablecloth, grab and crunch
Too late: toast is cold

Babies

The balls walk like ducks
Warm pink balls with wide big eyes
The need to have one

Kristina Bjorknas

The third myth of Johnny Lucifer

No the grass insistent sways
ask not us as our response
unsettles all. A river through
a ford indifference quotes.

The question stays and calls
back only with night when
the bonded warehouse flares
and salve is uncomplaining grass,

the fall that measures
us from it being a drop
of only feet to set him
free and walking upright home.

Leo Mellor

'Now is my fresh-vegetable waking up'

Now is my fresh-vegetable waking up,
My searing for flavour, my quick toss
In oil, my sharp-shock bucket of
Kitchen happiness.

At nine o'clock precisely this evening
I shall walk among the divine
Perfumed monsters in white iced
Crenellations.

The babies of sugar will run up and down
My arm and nymphets in party chocolate
Shall lure me into corners. There, I shall lie back
And think of salad.

Donovan Rees

Magdalene College, Christmas

Paul, get out your fiddle, night's growing;
the services are over, carols closed:
call a tune — yourself, the whistle, the drum —
laughter and listening and the party
growing warm; and John, call the dances.

And there's the shy and the bold
and the many who're both
the ones tattooed with purpose
and the many who don't know
there's the unwise and the learning
the lone and the lonely
the lads from in the pub
and the fiddler in the corner
carving at the strings

And one girl all in green, and silver tied
in blonde and her smile like Christmas apples: her steps
light as the smile, lighter than you'd think

And a rush of sable, ringlets, dark red
silk in a flow, a brooch of coiled silver
and barefoot grace beneath the skirt — poise
and pace and the slipping shirt baring her neck
and a young man with dark eyes turning
down the archways

And John, call the hornpipes
call the reels call a slipjig

never let us pause the dancing
tell each one what's his calling

call the lads pay them fool's gold
call the beams to frame a scaffold

call on the vicar and the master
call on the executioner

knot the cord and call the linchpin
call on Saint Mary Magdalene

call the grey light growing *Day*
call for mercy, call to pray.

Alaric Hall

Susan Pevensie

And she was called Queen Susan the Gentle.
"She always was a jolly sight too keen on being grown-up." — C.S. Lewis

The wireless announced the crash that night
while I dressed for a party at my friend's —
when they said 'Oxfordshire' I felt a jolt
of sickening recognition, stuffed my legs
into their scratchy nylons and thought — No,
why should it be their train? And if it was,
I'm sure they're all OK. I painted on
my best and bravest face, then someone knocked;
and when I saw the policeman in the hall
I thought I'd had the air punched from my lungs.

I gave names to the bodies, dry and cold
and broken like old dolls. They felt no pain,
officials told me, pity in their tones;
a young, well-spoken girl, with just enough
of beauty to be tragic, touched their hearts.
I lived on sympathy, in lieu of love;
in meetings with the lawyers about wills
and property, insurance and bequests,
I fluttered helpless as a butterfly
caught in their heavy nets, forced to be grave
when all my training was in how to flirt,
be frivolous and flighty. Now my wings
were clipped before I'd even learnt to glide,
and I was no-one's sister, no-one's child.

I married not long after, craving love,
and somebody to lift these sudden cares
upon his shoulders for me. As a boy,
he'd been the type that nurtures baby birds
and glues toys back together; I suspect

22

he thought he'd mend me too. I was transformed
into a weary matron overnight,
the way that God mocks all the dreams we have
by granting them, or giving something else
we never really wanted. Other girls
might plan for husbands, but I always thought
I'd be proud, free and single, as before;
back in that other world which was my home.

But Alice, surely, could not spend her life
still dreaming of the Wonderland she dreamed
so long ago; no-one can stay a child
and who would wish to? Children only weave
bright fantasies of what the world denies;
they have no power, must do as they are told,
and play's the only way they can escape
from our benign oppression.

                             It was like
a Monday morning waking when I found
myself in that back bedroom, beauty gone,
my royalty taken from me in a cloud
of greyness and utility. Once more
I was a gawky schoolgirl, and the birds
in England's trees sang songs that had no words.
I went back once, and breathed my proper air;
and then He said we'd never come again.
I ate no apple, disobeyed no law,
but I was exiled. Well, it does no good
to harp upon what's lost and can't return;
one's duty is to salvage what one can.
I made the best of this world, tried to catch
the shadows of the beauty that I'd lost —

though lips had never wanted painting there,
nor had I needed corsetry and wires
to cage me into something like the shape
I'd had when princes wooed me. After all,
poor Lucy was the clever one, not I.
She called me empty-headed; jealous of
the little I'd recaptured. She'd have laughed
if she'd have known sometimes I envied her
her closeness to our brothers, and her brains.

I couldn't bear to hear them reminisce,
back then, about the place we'd left behind;
do you think Eve would ever turn to press
her face against the gates of Eden, or
swap tales with Adam of how great it was
before the world was ruined? They might plan
on getting back, defying His decree;
their stubborn blindness riled me, though I laughed
and told them they should drop such childish things.
He'd said that we could never come again;
and I, for one, could never doubt His word.

And then a train crashed, one slow summer day,
and banished me from yet another world:
the giddy whirl of surfaces and fun
I'd crafted in the absence of my home,
where I had gossiped, giggled, and despised
the way my siblings clung to what was gone;
made my accommodation to the flawed,
imperfect universe where I was born.
It snatched from me the people that I loved;
and then I knew at last there was a God
who hated me, the way he'd hated Eve,

for being what he'd have me. All she did
was what she was commanded by the snake;
obedient to him, since all she knew
was doing what they told her. All I was
was pretty, silly Susan, father's pet;
if I must be brought low, it was enough
to have some dashing scoundrel break my heart,
or blot my reputation with the jibes
of jealous girlfriends. Little pins suffice
to stab a butterfly, and there's no call
to press a primrose with a juggernaut.

My husband's kind; our children, little dears —
I never wanted children — roam the fields.
I struggle not to love them overmuch
for one day I shall lose them. And sometimes
I whisper to the dogs it's safe to speak,
or listen to the sparrows, half-asleep
and puzzled I don't understand their song;
for when the sun rose at Cair Paravel
I heard them every morning, swapping news.
And once I had a dream of Aslan's fur;
my girlish head was buried in its gold,
warm gold, a solid halo which I breathed,
a power of strength and goodness. When I woke —
I think my life's curse lies in those three words —
I rubbed sleep from my eyes, and brushed my hair
(I never shall have beauty now) and went
downstairs to chop some apples for the pie.

Carolyn Smith

Subtraction

I cut my teeth teaching primary school maths
in the New Forest to a class
of thirteen (which was unlucky
for all of us).

The odd one out was a right little twat,
thick as pigshit, mouthy with it,
gaptoothed, spectacled, looped by
doughnuts of fat.

One morning he rolled in an hour late
with no satchel and a limp note
from his mum between chubby paws.
Well, that was that.

We'd spent Lesson One jumping through the basic
                                        hoops —
the creed of the times table and square roots —
and Lesson Two on fractions, in
six congruent groups,

finding the lowest common denominator.
We agreed he had to be got rid of.
And so the kids set about him,
right then and there;

caught him in a tightening dodecahedron,
gagged him with a football sock, brought him down
with a rounders bat to the gut,
a pump to the groin,

and an exercise book to the back of the head.
I finished him off with the blackboard.
It occurred to me at that point
that a problem shared

is a problem squared.

Sam Gilbert

Testing Surfaces

Travelling through Japan,
the Russian journalist Ovchinnicov
notes that the Japanese are
             'attracted to the darkened
             'tone of an old tree, the
             'ruggedness of a stone'.
There is, thus, he concludes,
some aesthetic value
taken on by that
which is old — *saba*:
             'an element of beauty', which
             'embodies the link between
             'art and nature'.
The dictionary, however,
defines *saba* as
             'mackerel'.

2

Saba: also the
largest city in
'Arabia Felix'
(a Roman province).

Saba Sabaoth:
City of Angels,
Rusty City,
Mackerel of Hosts;

The rusty city
teems with life,
the surface petrified:
saba sabaoth.

Its grains map out
windows, outlines,
the latenight phonecall:

'Mightn't it be kept
'out of the press?
'[a name] Please!' or else

'when we hunted
'through the great rooms
'for cigarettes'.

'A tract of quivering gray
'intelligent without purpose
'excitable without love'.

3

There is a house, around my way,
that Malevich never painted.
Perfectly symmetrical, from the front,
it thrusts out blank concrete
just as far as the layer of paint that
slices down its white border
and stops it. Frozen.

The lower two windows are boarded up
with wood of indeterminate beige,
making it seem all chin and brow.
A segment of sky has been cut out
in order that it might jut there,
shorn away for its bulldog face,
though nothing lies near but the hardmouthed road,

      the city is whose corroded teeth,
      a face of worn enamel.

Tom Perrin

'A lupine sky'

A lupine sky glues herself to the edges of my sightline
A great black tree grasps fingers at its scribbled outline
I balance bellyfirst on the magic carpet of a Motown bassline

In the softly spoken attic at the top of the third staircase
I lie drunk with Green and Gaye, Flack, Womack,
                              Jackson, Brown and Isaac Hayes
I try to roll a joint upon the speaker of the wonderbass

Give up and let my limbs drop in the whispered water
                              of the tide
Just think about a mind, it must be very like a mouth inside
I lap out like a wolfcub at the memory of you by my side

Robin French

Life Drawing

The studio is insulated.
It possesses its own life:
Its small breathings, and faint noises.
When charcoal and paper meet
There is no need for speech.

Hot air stands still.
Silence is pregnant
In both bodies.
Her body speaks
To him. She looks at him
Intensely. She watches herself
Being looked at. Whereas

He is a geographer — he is God. Meticulously, he is
Mapping out contours of each snow-capped hill
Tenderly, upon which
Each pink eye sleeps.
The artist
Scuttles nimbly across the virginal sheet,
Making a flat, mute body live.
It is also body making a hand live.

Love is still here.
There is love
Even for this sheet of paper:
New, fresh like a baby.
The artist loves this paper
As a housewife loves her fresh laundry.

Art has made the bodies live
Apart, but not so distant.
Her beauty lives not for the artist
As her eyes graze past him;
Nor he for her,
His eyes aroused by more
Or less, than her breasts and limbs.

His feelings spread and spill over his drawing
Of her. She watches each line form and move
To become like her.
She looks at the drawing getting more real, and then
Her own person shall become to herself a counterfeit,
And to the artist only skin.

Anon.

contributors

Contributors

Anon: the Publishers regret that they are unable to provide details of this Oxonian writer.

Kristina Bjorknas (Worcester College, Oxford) writes haiku at the rare moments when her thoughts stray away from her intriguing research in organic electroluminescence at the Department for Engineering Science. She was born in Finland and usually writes her haiku in Swedish or Finnish.

Heather Clark is writing a D.Phil on the Belfast Group poets at Lincoln College, Oxford. She is a graduate of Harvard University and Trinity College, Dublin, and a native of Cape Cod, Massachusetts. In 1999 she won the Martin Starkie Prize for Poetry, awarded by the Oxford University Poetry Society. Her story *Heart's Desire* appeared in the 1999 Short Stories May Anthology.

Robin French is a third-year student at Selwyn College, Cambridge, reading Italian and French. He is currently practising his Italian on Florentine women, and writing plays. A former Footlights leading man, he sports a *Shaft*-like afro.

Sam Gilbert is at Merton College, Oxford.

Alaric Hall (Magdalene College, Cambridge) owes great thanks to Cambridge's ASNaC department, whose boat he has been rocking now for three years. He also owes thanks to many individuals, but won't name names. His poem *Freya's* appeared in the 1998 Poetry May Anthology.

Emily Haworth-Booth won the Young National Poetry Competition in 1998, then studied for a year at Chelsea College of Art before starting an English degree at Clare College, Cambridge.

Lee Kern (ZZXPPQQFZZ....ZZZ FZZ,) H-ELLO. My name is Info-Bot.-Factual-Android. Glad you could make transmission connection — (Beep-Fizz KKPT) Sorry…static. Join me and my Red Time-Team as we voyage through space and time, in pursuit of History. (ZZZWhirrrr Pleep Alpha Alpha).

Leo Mellor was born in Brighton. He studied at King's College, Cambridge, graduating in 1999. His collection "marsh fear / fen tiger" is being published by Folio. He is currently living in Hokkaido, northern Japan. Critical works include articles on J.H. Prynne, David Jones, rock climbing and Japanese subcultures.

Tom Perrin (Corpus Christi College, Cambridge) used to be a Goth in Hertfordshire, but has bade farewell both to his past and to much of his hair since arriving in Cambridge. A confirmed dilettante and keen amateur concrete enthusiast, he found his poetic muse one sunny day atop a multi-storey car park.

Donovan Rees is a second-year studying English at St Hugh's College, Oxford. He is VP of the university Poetry Society and hopes to scrape his living writing.

Carolyn Smith was born in South Wales in 1977, and read English at Somerville College, Oxford. She is now working towards a DPhil on mid-Victorian women's poetry.

Michael Snediker received his BA from Williams College, and is currently finishing an M.Phil in American Literature at Cambridge. He will begin his Ph.D. at Johns Hopkins University next fall.

Benjamin Yeoh (an alumnus of Emmanuel College, Cambridge, and the student editor of the May Anthologies 1999) is currently on a Scholarship at Harvard where he is pursuing further work and research in experimental psychology, playwrighting, poetry and Americans. He hopes to return to England, some day, and somehow make some money.